dabblelab

CIRCUIT CREATIONS

MAKE CIRCUITS YOU CAN WEAR

Chris Harbo and Sarah L. Schuette

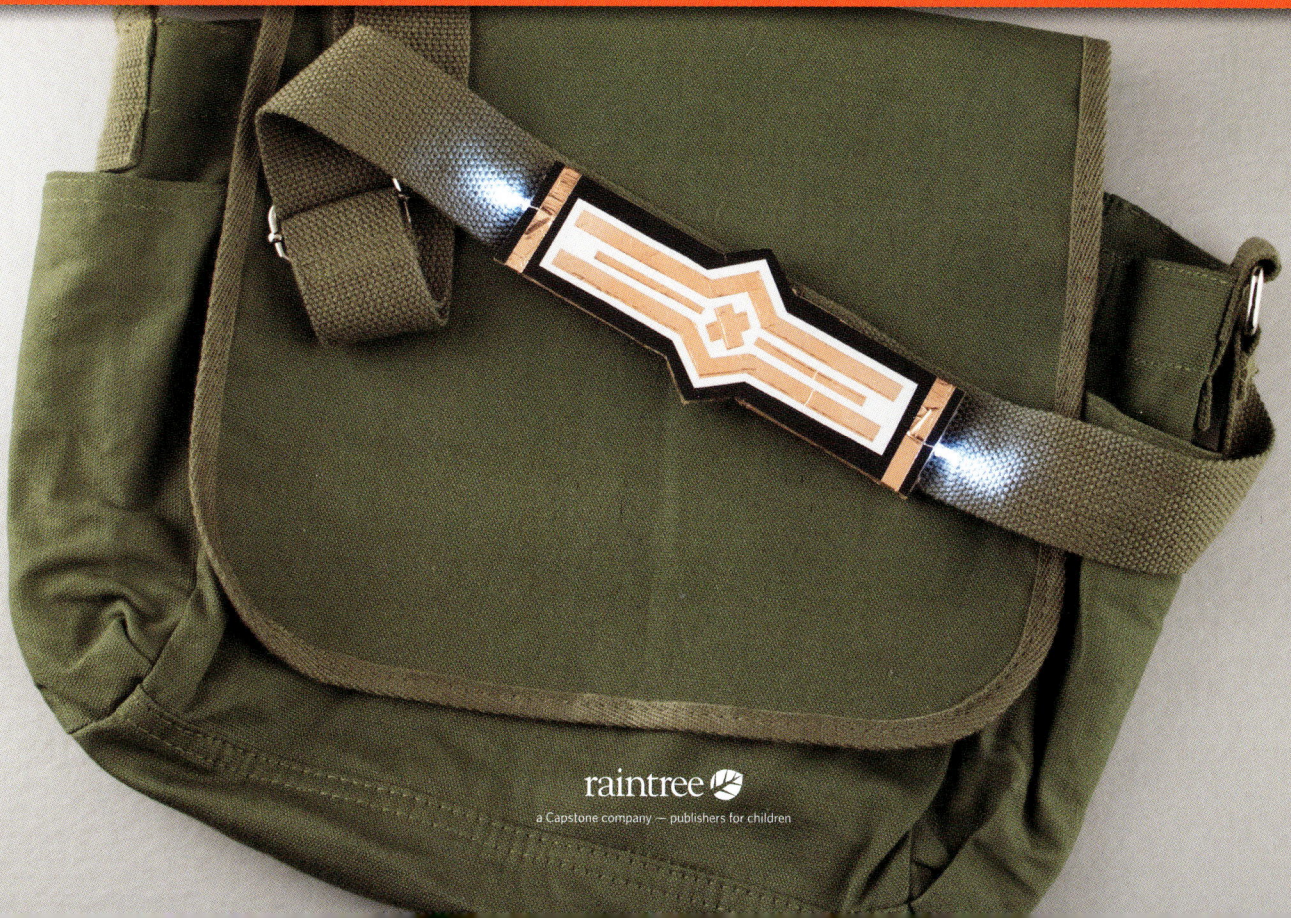

raintree

a Capstone company — publishers for children

Raintree is an imprint of Capstone Global Library Limited, a company incorporated in England and Wales having its registered office at 264 Banbury Road, Oxford, OX2 7DY – Registered company number: 6695582

www.raintree.co.uk
myorders@raintree.co.uk

Edited by Abby Colich
Designed by Juliette Peters
Original illustrations © Capstone Global Library Limited 2021
Picture research by Jo Miller
Production by Laura Manthe
Originated by Capstone Global Library Ltd
Printed and bound in India

978 1 4747 8657 7 (hardback)
978 1 4747 6788 0 (paperback)

British Library Cataloguing in Publication Data
A full catalogue record for this book is available from the British Library.

Acknowledgements
We would like to thank the following for permission to reproduce photographs: all photographs by Capstone: Karon Dubke; Marcy Morin and Sarah Schuette, Project Production; Heidi Thompson, Art Director
Design Elements: Capstone; Shutterstock: bygermina, rikkyall

Every effort has been made to contact copyright holders of material reproduced in this book. Any omissions will be rectified in subsequent printings if notice is given to the publisher.

All the internet addresses (URLs) given in this book were valid at the time of going to press. However, due to the dynamic nature of the internet, some addresses may have changed, or sites may have changed or ceased to exist since publication. While the author and publisher regret any inconvenience this may cause readers, no responsibility for any such changes can be accepted by either the author or the publisher.

CONTENTS

● ● ● ● ●

ELECTRIC FASHION

From wristwatches to headlamps, every electrical device you wear uses a circuit. But circuits aren't just for gear and gadgets you can buy in a shop. With a few basic materials, you can make several safe and simple circuits all by yourself. And once you do, you can easily pair them with a variety of wearable accessories. From glowing headlamps and necklaces to gadget goggles and propeller hats, get ready to add some fun flash to your fashions with the power of circuits!

SAFETY TIPS

While working with circuits and electricity, keep these important safety tips in mind.

- All projects should be done with adult supervision.
- Always disconnect your circuits when not in use.
- Never put batteries in your mouth.
- Never experiment with plug sockets.

WHAT IS A CIRCUIT?

In its simplest form, a circuit is a looping path that an electric current flows through. For this path to carry electricity, it often uses four main components. These are a power source, a conductor, a load and a controller.

Common power sources for circuits are batteries and plug sockets. A conductor is any material, such as metal wire, that can carry electricity. A load is a device, such as a light bulb or motor, that uses the electricity to work. And a controller is a switch that starts or stops the flow of electricity.

For any circuit to work, all four components must be connected in an unbroken loop. When you turn on a torch's switch, a closed circuit is created. Electricity flows from the battery, along a wire, through the switch, to the light bulb and back to the battery. When you flick the torch's switch off, a break in the circuit stops the flow of electricity to turn the light bulb off.

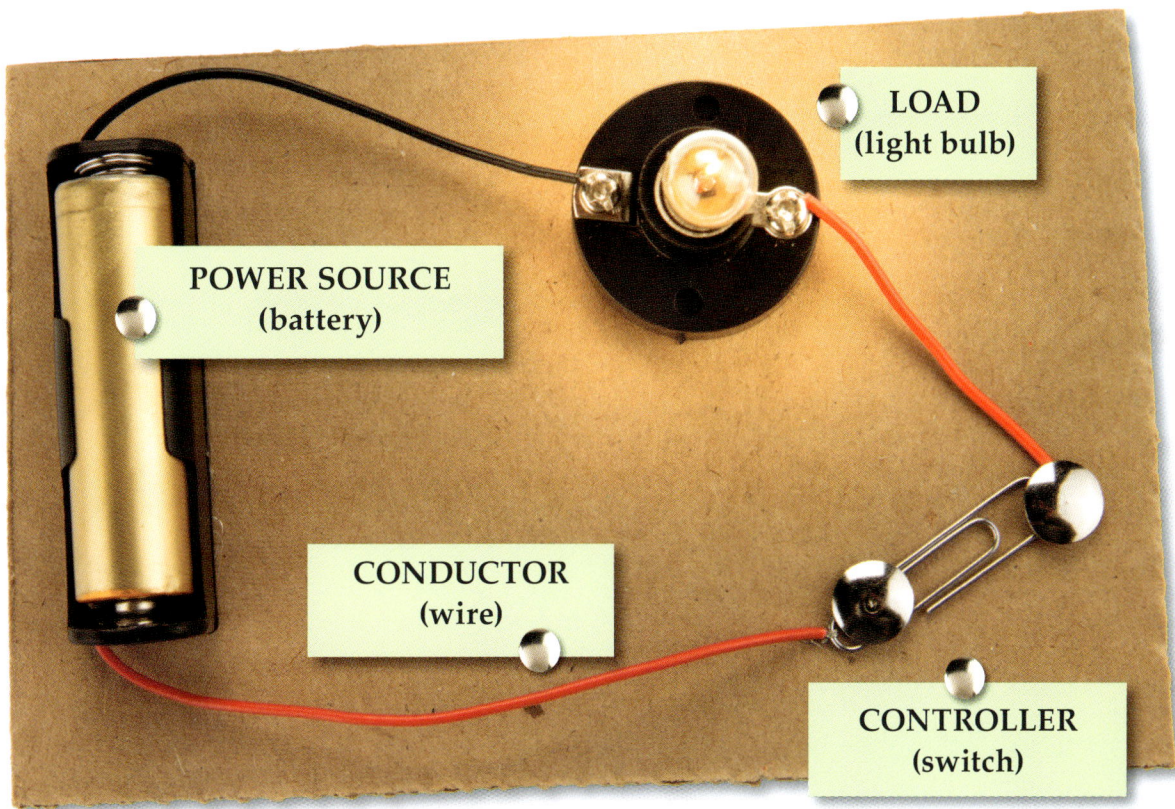

LOAD
(light bulb)

POWER SOURCE
(battery)

CONDUCTOR
(wire)

CONTROLLER
(switch)

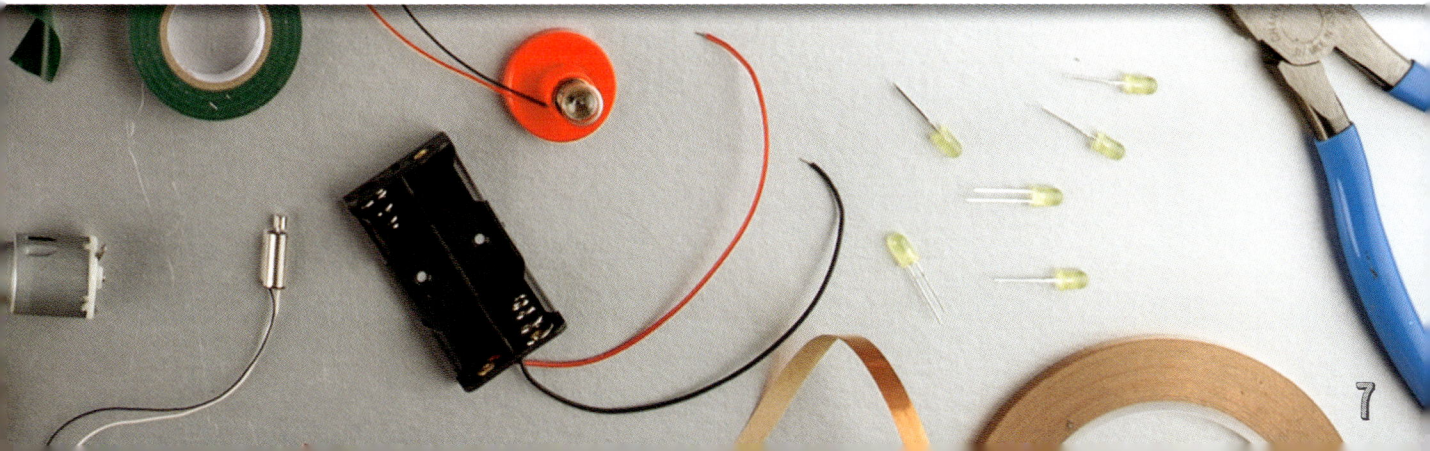

SIMPLE CIRCUITS

Now that you know how circuits work, you can practise connecting them. Then use your imagination to add circuits to common objects and create new things. You can make circuits with a variety of batteries, bulbs and other easy-to-find items. Use what you have available.

WHAT YOU NEED

AA battery in holder with lead wires
bulb socket and bulb
small screwdriver
insulated wire
wire stripper
2 metal drawing pins
cardboard
metal paper clip
LED
CR2032 button battery
electrical tape

MAKE IT!

LIGHT UP A LIGHT BULB

1. Connect the black wire from the battery holder to one side of the light bulb socket. If the socket has screws, use them to hold the wire in place.

2. Repeat with the red wire and the other side of the socket. The light bulb will light up!

ADD A SWITCH

1. Connect the black wire from the battery holder to one side of the light bulb socket.

2. Cut a piece of wire. Use the wire stripper to strip both ends. Connect one end of the wire to the open side of the socket. Wrap the other end of the wire around a drawing pin. Press the drawing pin into the cardboard.

3. Connect the red wire from the battery holder to the end of a metal paper clip. Press the second drawing pin through the paper clip and into the cardboard. This drawing pin should be a short distance from the first drawing pin.

4. Move the paper clip to open and close the circuit and turn the light bulb on and off.

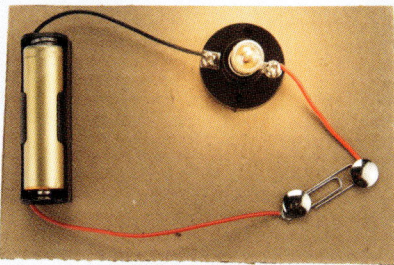

LIGHT UP AN LED

1. Slide an LED bulb onto a button battery. The long leg should touch the positive (+) side of the battery. The short leg should touch the negative (-) side.

2. Wrap electrical tape around the battery to hold the LED in place.

TIP!

Cut a small piece from a plastic lid. Slide it under an LED leg to turn the light off. Remove it to turn it back on.

STRIPPING WIRES

Before you begin making circuits, practise stripping wires. To strip, or remove, the coating on the end of a wire, use a wire stripper. Line up the wire size with the same size hole on the stripper. Press down lightly to cut into the coating without cutting the wire. Then pull the stripper away from your body.

HANDY HEADLAMP

Never dread the dark again. Build a handy headlamp that keeps your hands free during all of your night-time adventures.

WHAT YOU NEED

CR2032 button battery
LED
scissors
plastic lid
electrical tape
domed lid from a plastic cup
cardboard (optional)
foldback clip
hat

MAKE IT!

1. Slide the button battery between the legs of the LED. The long leg should touch the positive (+) side. The short leg should touch the negative (-) side.

2. Cut a small piece of plastic from a lid. Slide it under one leg of the LED. Slide the plastic piece in and out to turn the bulb off and on.

3. Wrap the circuit in several layers of electrical tape.

4. Place the bulb through the hole in the domed lid and secure the circuit using electrical tape. If the hole in the lid is too large for the bulb, cut a piece of cardboard the same size as the hole. Tape it inside the lid and cut a slit for the bulb to slide through.

5. Use the foldback clip to attach the lamp to your favourite hat. Slide the plastic piece out of the circuit to switch the lamp on.

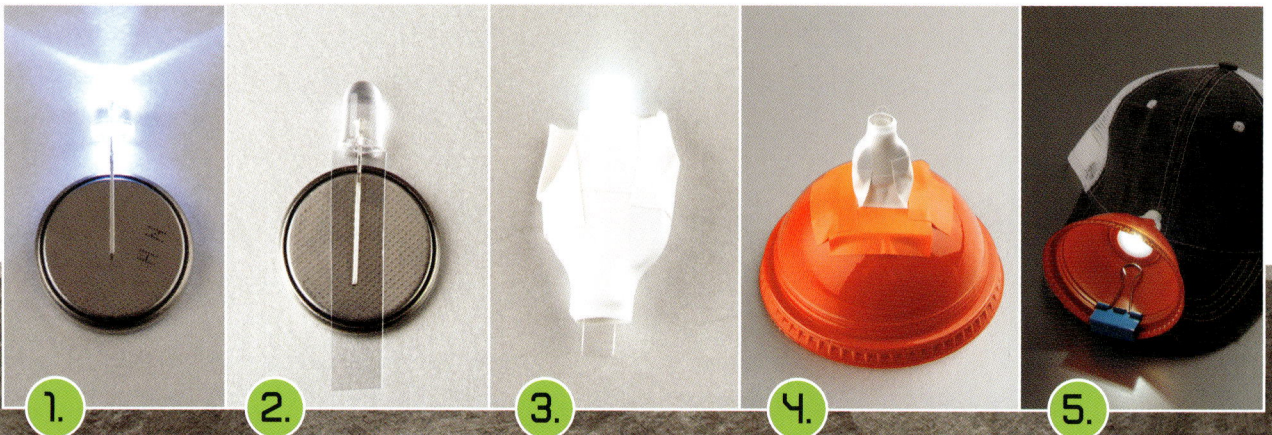

1. 2. 3. 4. 5.

Now that you've built the handy headlamp, reinvent it! Here are just two ways to do this.

TECH LIGHT ●●●●●

Shed a little light on the subject while using your laptop or mobile phone. Simply glue a mini clothes peg to the lid instead of using the foldback clip. Then attach the light to the edge of your laptop or phone. It can light up your workspace or serve as a clever selfie light.

LIGHT YOUR PATH! ●●●●●

Don't stumble and take a tumble in the dark. Turn your handy headlamp into a boot lamp instead. Once again, just glue a mini clothes peg to the lid instead of using the foldback clip. Then clip the light to the top of your boots or shoes to light your path. No more stubbed toes!

SHINING SEASHELL NECKLACE

Brighten up any outfit with just a circuit and a seashell. This nautical necklace is sure to get you plenty of oohs and aahs!

WHAT YOU NEED

CR2032 button battery
LED bulb
scissors
plastic lid
electrical tape
seashell
hot glue gun
coloured craft wire
needle-nose pliers
jump ring
leather cord

MAKE IT!

1. Slide the button battery between the legs of the LED. The long leg should touch the positive (+) side. The short leg should touch the negative (-) side.

2. Cut a small piece of plastic from a lid. Slide it under one leg of the LED. Slide the plastic piece in and out to turn the bulb off and on.

3. Wrap the circuit in several layers of electrical tape.

4. Glue the circuit inside the seashell.

5. Wrap the craft wire around the shell and make a loop in the wire at the top.

6. Use needle-nose pliers to attach a jump ring to the loop in the wire. Then thread the leather cord through the jump ring.

3.

4.

5.

6.

Don't have a shell? Use a piece of driftwood instead. What other natural objects could you use?

GADGET GOGGLES

Get into gear with a groovy pair of gadget goggles! With a built-in light, tape measure and more, there's no limit to what you can invent while wearing these spectacular specs.

WHAT YOU NEED

safety goggles with elastic band
hot glue gun
2 metal lid rings
light bulb socket and bulb
small wood block (optional)
AA battery holder with lead wires
mini tape measure
retractable card holder with an
    attached pen
small screwdriver
AA battery

MAKE IT!

1. Remove the elastic band from the safety goggles and put it aside. Glue two metal lid rings to the front of the goggles.

2. Glue a light bulb socket on top of the goggles. Add a small wood block to the bottom if you want the light to sit higher. Glue the AA battery holder near the light bulb socket.

3. Glue a mini tape measure to one side of the goggles. Then glue a retractable card holder with a pen attached to the other side of the goggles.

4. Connect the wires from the battery holder to the screws on the light bulb socket. Use a small screwdriver to tighten the screws.

5. Add the battery to the holder. The light bulb will light up.

6. Reattach the elastic band to the goggles and adjust as needed. Try out your new gadget goggles!

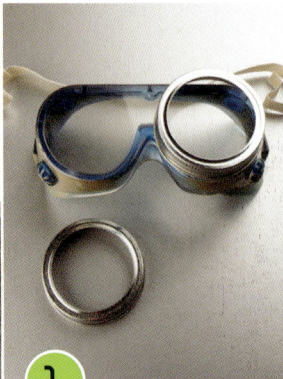

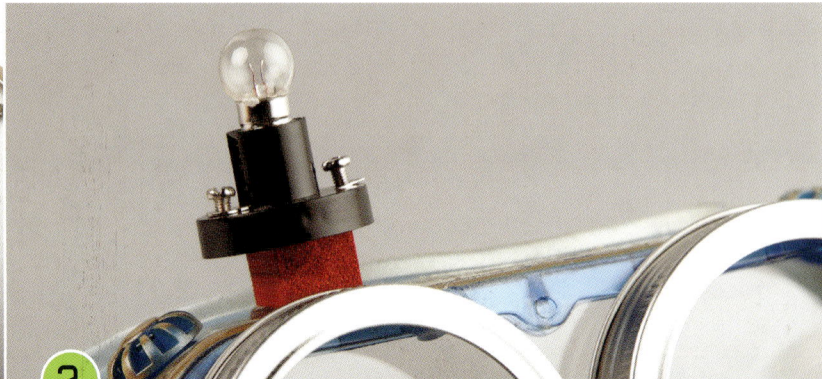

DECORATE IT!

Make attachments for your goggles. Use a wire with a clip to add a magnifying glass. Move the magnifying glass to the side when you don't need it. What other tools do you often use? How could you attach them?

CIRCUIT BOARD JEWELLERY

What can you do with all those spare parts from your circuit creations? Turn them into these wonderful wearables!

WHAT YOU NEED

4 small circuit boards
circuit board button switches
insulated wire
circuit board resistors
electrical tape
bracelet form
hot glue gun
scissors
jump ring
fish hook earring wire
needle-nose pliers
wire stripper
necklace chain or leather cording
ring form

MAKE IT!

BRACELET

1. Decorate a rectangular piece of circuit board with circuit board button switches, scraps of insulated wire and circuit board resistors. Bend the wires and prongs that poke out of the back of the circuit board to secure these pieces in place.

2. Cover the back of the circuit board with electrical tape.

3. Hot glue the board to the bracelet form.

EARRINGS

1. Cut a circuit board diagonally to create two triangle-shaped pieces.

2. Repeat step 1 from the bracelet with both triangular circuit boards.

3. Use needle-nose pliers to attach a jump ring to a hole near the point of one triangle. Then attach a fish hook earring wire to the jump ring. Repeat this step with the other triangle.

4. Cover the backs of both circuit boards with electrical tape.

BRACELET

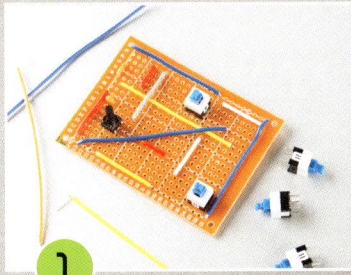

1.

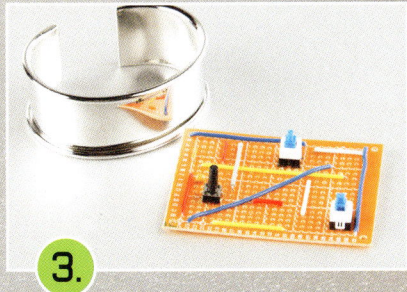

3.

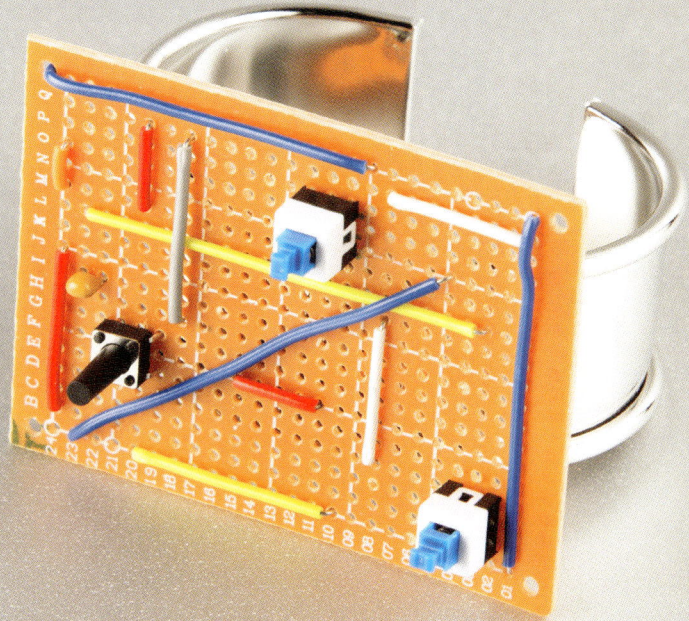

EARRINGS

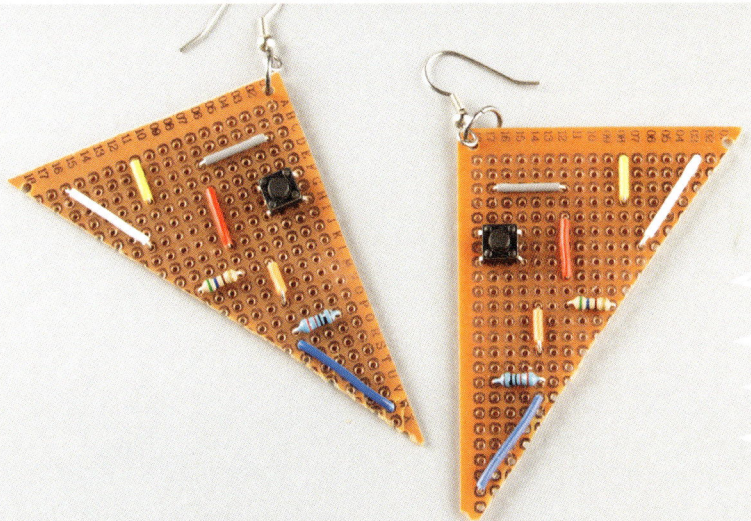

1.

2.

3.

4.

TURN THE PAGE.

19

NECKLACE

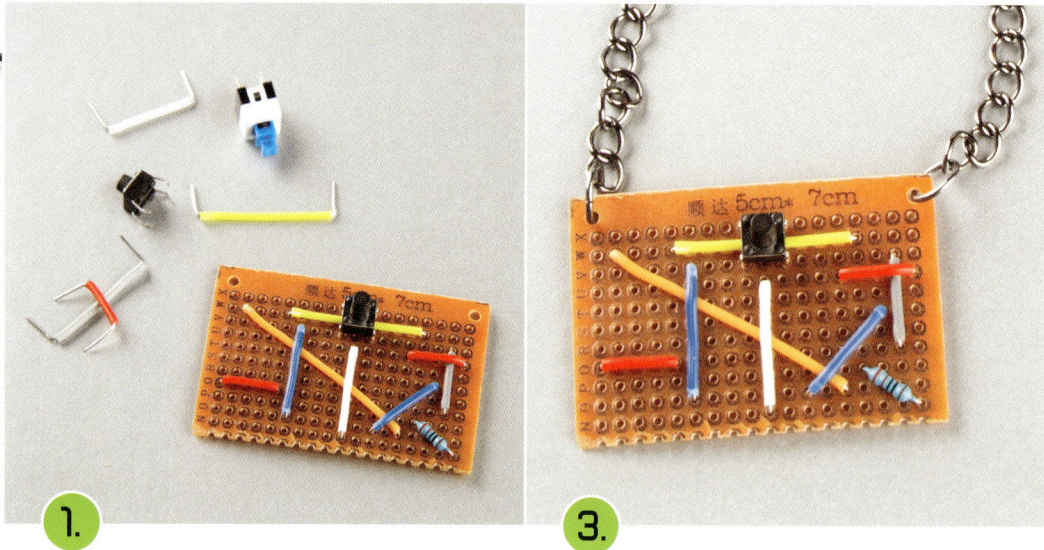

1.

3.

NECKLACE

1. Repeat step 1 from the bracelet with a rectangular piece of circuit board.

2. Cover the back of the circuit board with electrical tape.

3. Slide a necklace chain or leather cording through two holes in the circuit board to make a necklace.

RING

1. Repeat step 1 from the bracelet with a small square piece of circuit board.

2. Cover the back of the circuit board with electrical tape.

3. Glue the circuit board to a ring form.

RING

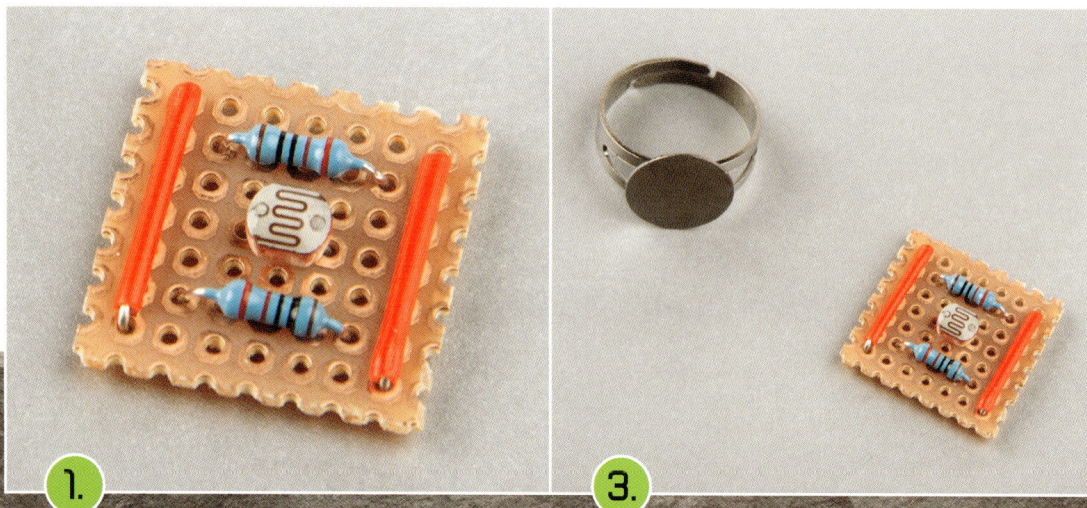

1.

3.

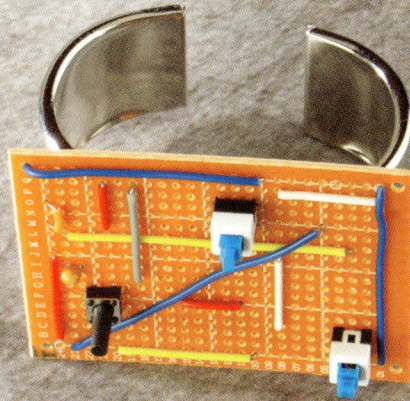

TOOL BELT AND LIGHT

All great circuit makers need a place to keep their tools. Design this handy tool belt so you never lose your tools again. Then add a homemade tool light to your tool belt so you can always find your tools – even in the darkest work areas!

WHAT YOU NEED

hot glue gun
leather or fabric strips
apron (any size)
plastic tubing
binder clip
electrical tape
light bulb circuit and socket with
    lead wires
domed lid from a cup
cardboard tube
AA batteries in holder with lead wires
    and switch

MAKE IT!

TOOL BELT

1. Glue strips of leather or fabric to the apron to make extra pockets and straps for your circuit-making tools.

2. Loop a piece of plastic tubing and secure it with a binder clip.

3. Add several rolls of electrical tape to the plastic tubing and clip it to the apron.

4. Store your wire strippers and extra wires in the pockets.

1.

2.

3.

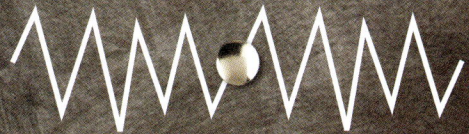

TURN THE PAGE.

TOOL LIGHT

1. Glue the light bulb socket into the hole in the plastic lid.

2. Glue the end of the cardboard tube to the lid, letting the socket wires hang down the tube.

3. Connect the red wire from the bulb socket to the black wire on the battery holder. Then connect the remaining two black and red wires together. Wrap the wire connections in electrical tape.

4. Tape the battery holder to the side of the tube.

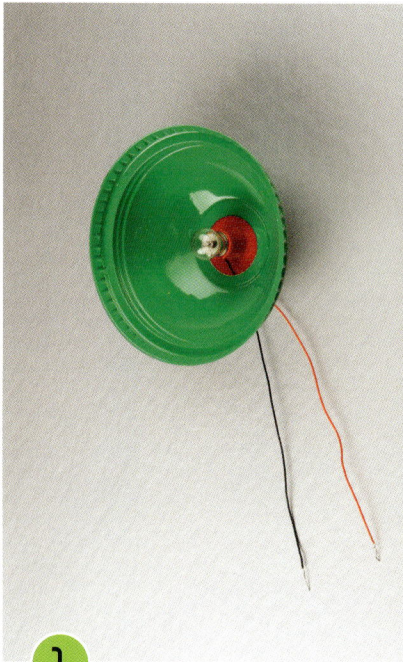

1.

2.

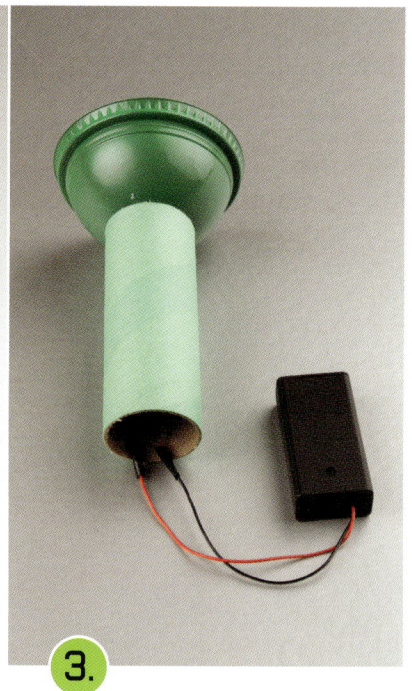

3.

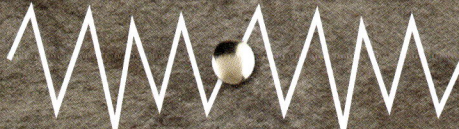

CHANGE IT UP!

Want to hang your tool light on your
tool belt? Use a craft knife or hole
punch to poke a hole in the side of the
tool light's tube. Then slide a long piece
of insulated wire through the hole.
Twist the ends of the wires together
around the tubing on your tool belt.

SIMPLE CONDUCTOR CIRCUITS

Graphite, copper, foil and other elements are good conductors for electricity. Electricity can flow through them, and they can be used to make paths for electricity. These paths are called traces. The best way to practise these circuits is on paper. Once you learn the basics, you can experiment with them on other surfaces.

WHAT YOU NEED

graphite pencil (2B or harder)
paper
LEDs
clear tape
9-volt battery
CR2032 button battery
copper tape

MAKE IT!

GRAPHITE CIRCUIT

1. With the graphite pencil, draw two parallel lines. Mark the ends of one line with positive (+) symbols. Then mark the other line with negative (-) symbols.

2. Open the legs of the LED. Tape each leg to one end of your lines. The long leg should touch the line with the positive (+) symbol. The short leg should touch the line with the negative (-) symbol.

3. Place the connection ports of the 9-volt battery on the other end of your lines. Match up the positive and negative ports of the battery to the markings on your drawing.

4. The LED will light up if the circuit is connected correctly. You may need to check the circuit in a dark place. The LED will be dimmer than lights from other circuits.

COPPER TAPE CIRCUIT

1. Use the graphite pencil to sketch a circuit path with two openings.

2. Remove the backing of the copper tape. Stick the copper tape on top of your sketch.

3. Spread the legs of the LED and tape them to the copper tape at one of the circuit's openings. One leg should connect to each end of copper tape.

4. At the second opening, place a button battery on top of one end of the copper tape. Then fold the corner of the paper over so the other end of the copper tape touches the top of the battery. Watch the LED light up.

CIRCUIT PENS AND PAINT

Experimenting with circuit writer pens and paint can be a lot of fun. Circuit pens can be found in craft shops. They work by drawing over the top of your graphite sketches. Once your traced lines are dry, just connect a battery and LED and watch the LED light up.

Circuit paint can be made by mixing the same amounts of liquid graphite powder and acrylic paint. Once again, just trace over your graphite circuits with the conductive paint, let it dry and then hook up your components.

TIP!

Before you use copper tape, cut a small piece and remove the backing. Does the tape look the same on both sides? If it does, then both sides of the tape are conductive. Some copper tape is only conductive on one side. Be very careful with copper tape. The edges can be sharp.

CONDUCTIVE THREAD

Conductive thread can also carry electricity because it is made with metals that conduct electricity. This type of thread is mostly used to make flexible circuits for textiles. Here's how to make a simple circuit with conductive thread.

WHAT YOU NEED

LED
sewable button battery holder
felt
scissors
conductive thread
sewing needle
CR2032 button battery

MAKE IT!

1. Place the LED bulb on one side of the piece of felt and the sewable button battery holder on the other.

2. Cut a length of conductive thread.

3. Tie one end of the conductive thread to the long leg of the LED.

4. Thread a needle with the other end of the conductive thread.

5. Sew a line of simple stitches from the LED to the positive (+) tab of the sewable button battery holder. Tie the end of the thread to the positive tab.

6. Cut a second piece of thread. Repeat steps 3 to 5 to connect the short leg of the LED to the negative (-) tab on the sewable button battery holder.

7. Insert the button battery into the holder and the LED will light up!

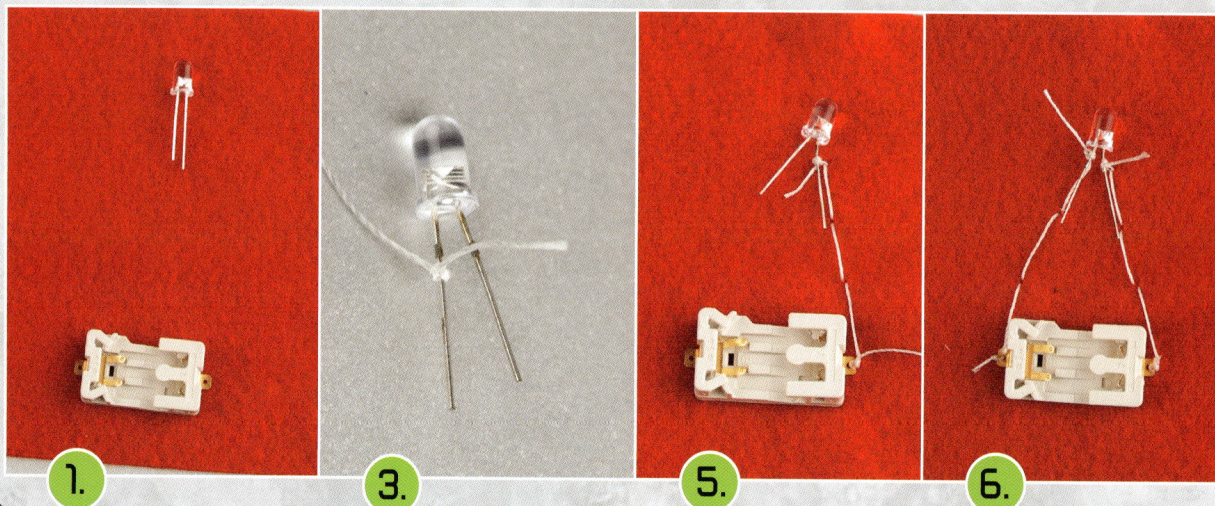

1.

3.

5.

6.

YOU CAN BE A CIRCUIT

Every time you swipe across a touchscreen, your body becomes a circuit! Sometimes electricity can even flow through your body and you become a conductor. Your finger completes the circuit for the electronic device you are trying to use. For a glove to work on a touchscreen, it needs to complete a circuit with your finger. You can use conductive thread to complete the circuit.

BAG STRAP BLING

Change a school bag from boring to brilliant. Add bling to the straps with a simple copper tape circuit.

WHAT YOU NEED

- scissors
- coloured card
- bag with cross-body strap
- pencil
- copper tape
- hot glue gun
- cardboard
- CR2032 button battery
- 2 LEDs
- name tag pin

MAKE IT!

1. Cut a piece of coloured card that is the same width as the strap on the bag. Sketch a design on this card and cover it with copper tape.

2. Glue the card to a piece of cardboard. Turn the cardboard over.

3. Glue a name tag pin to the back of the cardboard.

4. Line the back of the cardboard with two strips of copper tape. Snip one strip in half. Allow one half to lie on top of a button battery. Allow the other half to lie beneath the battery.

5. Connect LEDs to the copper strips at the ends of the cardboard. The long legs should go under one strip and the short legs under the other. The LEDs will light up.

6. Attach the cardboard piece to the bag strap with a name tag pin.

1.

3.

4.

COOL BOOK BAG

Give an old tote bag new life with lights! Then carry your books to school or the library in style with a flashy bag.

WHAT YOU NEED

canvas tote bag
paint pen
LEDs
needle
conductive thread
sewable button battery holder
CR2032 button battery

MAKE IT!

1. Draw your favourite constellation on the outside of the bag with a paint pen. Make dots for stars around the constellation.

2. Poke the legs of LEDs through the dots and canvas to look like stars.

3. Thread the needle with a long piece of conductive thread. Tie the two ends together. Place the sewable battery holder on the inside of the bag, near the first star in your constellation. Stitch through the positive (+) terminal of the battery holder to secure it to the bag.

4. Stitch to and over the long leg on the first LED. Keep stitching to connect all of the long LED legs. Finish the last stitch on the inside of the bag, and then tie the thread in a knot.

5. Repeat step 3 with another piece of conductive thread. This time connect the negative terminal of the battery holder to the short LED legs. When finished, tie off the thread on the inside of the bag.

6. Add the button battery to the holder, and your stars will glow!

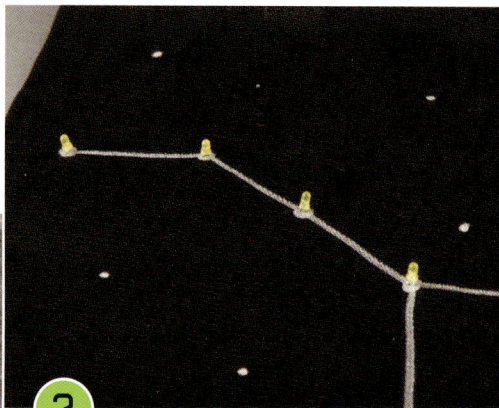

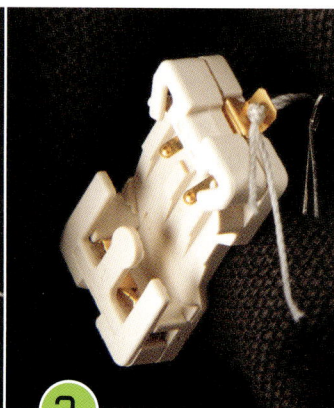

2.

3.

4.

TECH GLOVES

Don't let cold weather keep you unconnected. Build a pair of tech gloves that not only work with a touchscreen, but also help you hang onto your earbuds.

WHAT YOU NEED

scissors
felt
needle
conductive thread
woolly gloves
felt-tip pen
adhesive hook-and-loop dots
earbuds

MAKE IT!

1. Cut a small circle out of the felt that is about the size of your fingertip. Thread the needle with conductive thread and knot the two ends together. Push the needle through the middle of the felt circle.

2. Use a felt-tip pen to draw a burst shape on the felt. Use the marker lines to sew a burst shape with the conductive thread. When you've finished, make a knot on the back to keep it from unravelling.

3. Insert a marker into the finger of the glove. Then sew the felt circle onto the fingertip, burst shape out.

4. Sew a strap of felt to the back of the glove. Add adhesive hook-and-loop dots to the strap, and use it to hold your earbuds.

1.

2.

3.

4.

LIGHT-UP STYLUS AND TECH SCARF

Add function to your fashion. Build a light-up stylus that tucks perfectly into the clever pockets of a tech scarf. Turn the stylus around and it becomes a light-up pencil. Now, that's technical!

WHAT YOU NEED

felt
scissors
felt-tip pen
needle
conductive thread
pencil with eraser
elastic band
LED
CR2032 button battery
plastic lid
electrical tape
small plastic cup
hot glue gun
small clothes peg
old scarf

MAKE IT!

LIGHT-UP STYLUS

1. Cut a circle out of felt about the size of a roll of electrical tape. Use a felt-tip pen to trace around a pencil eraser on the centre of the circle.

2. Thread the needle with conductive thread. Push the needle through the middle of the felt circle.

3. Sew stitches on top of the marker lines. Make a knot on the back to keep it from unravelling.

4. Wrap the felt piece onto the pencil eraser and secure with an elastic band.

5. Slide a button battery between the legs of an LED. The long leg should touch the positive (+) side, and the short leg should touch the negative (-) side.

6. Cut a small rectangle out of the plastic lid. Slide it under one leg of the LED, then wrap the circuit in several layers of electrical tape. Slide the plastic piece in and out to turn the bulb off and on.

7. Cut a hole in the bottom of the plastic cup. Trim the cup into a shade for the light. Push the LED from the circuit through the hole in the cup.

8. Glue a clothes peg to the light and clip it to the pencil. Now you can have extra light while using your devices, or turn the light around to write at night!

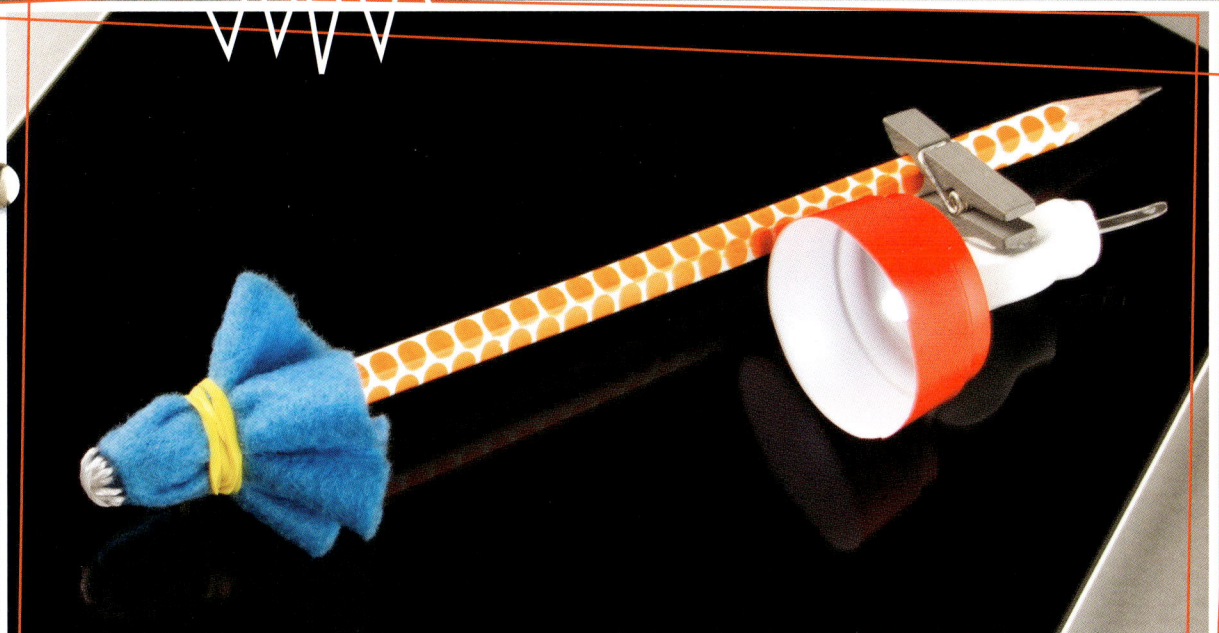

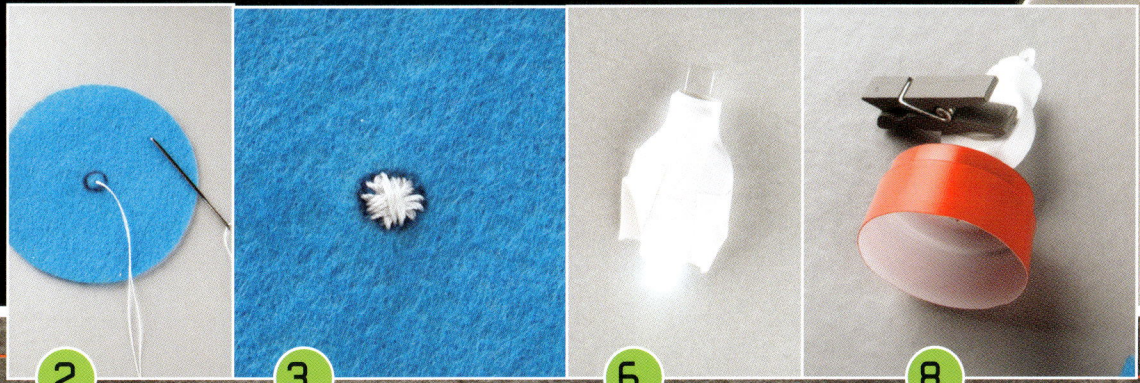

2.   3.   6.   8.

TECH SCARF

1. Cut shapes out of felt.

2. Glue them to the scarf as pockets.

3. Use the pockets to store your stylus, tech gloves, phone or small tablet.

1.

2.

MOVING CIRCUITS

Now that you can connect simple circuits, let's make circuits that move! Batteries store energy for use when you need it. Magnets can be used to make electricity. They can work independently or together in the circuits you create.

WHAT YOU NEED

low-speed hobby motor
AA batteries in holder with switches
    and lead wires
mini vibrating motor
CR2032 button battery
neodymium magnets
AA battery
copper wire
needle-nose pliers

MAKE IT!

POWER A MOTOR

1. Connect the black wire from the battery holder to the red wire from the motor. Then connect the remaining two wires the same way.

2. Wrap and secure both connections with electrical tape.

3. Switch on the battery pack and watch the shaft on the motor spin!

CONNECT A MINI VIBRATING MOTOR

1. Connect the black wire from the mini vibrating motor to the negative (-) side of the button battery. Secure the connection with electrical tape.

2. Connect the red wire from the motor to the positive (+) side of the battery. Watch the motor wiggle!

MAKE A HOMOPOLAR MOTOR

1. Stack the neodymium magnets on top of each other.

2. Place the AA battery on top of the magnets, positive (+) side down.

3. Wrap the copper wire down around the battery to make a coil. The coil should be loose around the battery and magnet stack.

4. Use needle-nose pliers to bend a small dip at the top of your wire coil.

5. Balance the dip on top of the battery and watch the wire coil spin!

MINI JUNK BOT

Try making some miniature junk bots that you can wear. You'll giggle as these bots wiggle!

WHAT YOU NEED

vibrating motor
CR2032 button battery
electrical tape
craft wire
pencil
awl
plastic bottle cap
googly eyes and other craft materials
lanyard with clip

MAKE IT!

1. Connect the red wire from the vibrating motor to the positive (+) side of the button battery. Secure with electrical tape.

2. Connect the black wire from the motor to the negative (-) side of the battery. The motor will wiggle. Disconnect while you build the rest of the project.

3. Coil pieces of craft wire around a pencil. Remove the pencil.

4. Use an awl to poke a hole in the cap. Slide the ends of the wire coil into the hole. Bend the wire ends inside the cap to hold them in place.

5. Stick googly eyes to the coiled wire or the side of the bottle cap. Add any other small craft decorations you like.

6. Tape the motor and battery under the cap with electrical tape.

7. Reconnect the black wire to the battery and secure with electrical tape. Clip coiled wire to a lanyard and wear your wiggly bot!

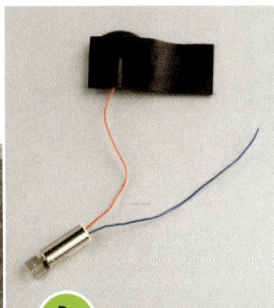

1.   3.   4.   6.

THROWING STAR SPINNER SHOES

Get your kicks with a cool pair of shoes. These ninja-inspired spinner shoes are sure to get everyone's attention!

WHAT YOU NEED

scissors
cardboard
2 low-speed hobby motors with lead wires
electrical tape
skewer
2 toy wheels or plastic propellers
2 AA battery holders with lead wires
    and switches
hot glue gun
2–4 AA batteries

MAKE IT!

1. Cut four star shapes out of cardboard. In the centre of two of the stars, cut holes the same size as the motors.

2. Slide the motors through the holes and secure with electrical tape.

3. Poke a hole in the centre of the other stars with a skewer. Slide the stars onto each motor's shaft.

4. Add a toy wheel or plastic propeller to the end of each motor's shaft.

5. Connect the black wire from the battery holders to the red wires on the motors. Then connect the remaining red and black wires for each motor and battery holder. Wrap all of the connections in electrical tape.

6. Glue the battery holders and the spinners to the shoes. Switch on the holders to turn the spinners on.

1.

2.

4.

HELI-HAT

No one ever said you can't have fun and stay safe at the same time. Just give this helicopter hard hat a whirl!

WHAT YOU NEED

hot glue gun
small wooden block
low-speed hobby motor with lead wires
plastic bottle cap
scissors
cardboard
wooden skewer
construction hard hat
AA batteries in holder with lead
   wires and switch
electrical tape

MAKE IT!

1. Glue a small wooden block to the bottom of the motor. Glue the block and motor to the inside of a plastic bottle cap.

2. Connect the black wire from the battery holder to the red motor wire. Then connect the remaining red and black wires. Wrap the connections with electrical tape.

3. Cut out a propeller shape from the cardboard. Poke a hole in the centre of the propeller with a wooden skewer. Insert the motor's shaft into the hole in the propeller.

4. Glue the bottle cap to the top of the hard hat.

5. Glue the battery pack to the back of the hat. Add strips of electrical tape and plastic propellers to the hat as decorations.

2. 3. 4.

GLOSSARY

battery container holding chemicals that store and create electricity

button battery small, disc-shaped battery

component part of a machine or system

conductor material that lets heat, electricity or sound travel easily through it

controller switch or other mechanism in a circuit that starts and stops the flow of electricity

current flow of electrons through an object

gadget small tool that does a particular job

graphite black or grey mineral in pencils; graphite is the part of a pencil used for writing

LED type of light; LED stands for light-emitting diode

load device to which power is delivered

magnet piece of metal that attracts iron or steel

nautical of or concerning sailors and ships

neodymium magnet very strong, permanent magnet made up of the elements neodymium, iron and boron

stylus pen-like instrument used to enter information on electronic devices

switch part of a circuit that turns electrical objects on or off; a switch creates a gap in a circuit

textile fabric or cloth that has been woven or knitted

FIND OUT MORE

A Beginner's Guide to Circuits: Nine Simple Projects with Lights, Sounds, and More!
Øyvind Nydal Dahl (No Starch Press, 2018)

Electronics Projects for Beginners (Hands-on Projects for Beginners), Tammy Enz
(Raintree, 2019)

Inventor Lab: Awesome Builds for Smart Makers, Jack Challoner (DK Children, 2019)

WEBSITES

bbc.co.uk/bitesize/topics/zq99q6f
Find out more about circuits, how to adapt them and learn the symbols used to
represent each component.

dkfindout.com/uk/science/electricity/circuits/
Learn about the different types of circuits, experiment with different conductors
and insulators and take a quiz to test your knowledge.

MAKE **ART** WITH CIRCUITS

MAKE **CIRCUITS** YOU CAN **WEAR**

MAKE **CIRCUITS** THAT **GLOW** OR **GO**

MAKE **GAMES** WITH **CIRCUITS**